EXECUTIVE SUMMARY

Over the course of a 6-year period (2015-2020), the results of this unique, real estate research project, conclusively showed that a residential sales methodology, which was centred around high-calibre property styling, **provides significant, and commercially measurable improvements in the sales price and sales speed** of residential property sales.

It is important to note that the majority of Greater Brisbane Suburbs experienced little to no price growth over the multi-year study period. The significant 'out-performance' (suburb to suburb) of the sales approach employed in this study provides substantial weight to the proposition that **the study's high-performance sales results were a direct function of its 'presentation-centric' sales approach** and not just a result of a 'run-away' friendly marketplace or suburb.

Graph 1.4 provides further confirmation of the beneficial difference generated by a presentation-centric sales approach. This graph highlights that the approach adopted in this study illustrates **sales speeds 5 to 6 times faster than the overall Brisbane market sales timeframes for the entire period of this project.**

Throughout the course of this research project **a consistent sales approach was employed** where all aspects of the presentation and marketing remained unchanged for each property campaign in order to test the impact of a presentation-centric sales approach on a wide variety of homes (144) in a wide variety of locations (62 suburbs).

> "The evidence supporting the benefits of the sales methodology used in this study, and its ability to produce **CONSISTENTLY HIGHER PRICES AND FASTER SALES TIMES**, is overwhelming."
>
> – P. Coulson, President, Interior Design Association

- The **majority (66%) of all sales were sold within the first 14 days** of each property campaign.
- **87% of all sales were sold within the first 30 days** of each property campaign.
- The **average Days-On-Market was just 14 days** for the entire 144 property sales over the 6 year period.
- The **median Days-On-Market was just 9 days** for the entire 144 property sales over the 6 year period.
- The **average price premium** across all sales was **$69,017** (7.3% above-market).
- **63%** of all 144 consecutive sales were **sold for an above-market price premium of 3-15%.**
- The average sales price was $1,026,309 across the 144 sales with a total sales value of $147,088,500.

OBJECTIVES & METHODOLOGY

The objective of this multi-year retrospective observational study was to assess the commercial merits of a presentation-centric sales process. This required a high level of **'sales process consistency'** in order to eliminate random outcomes and to ensure that the same approach was applied to all types of homes in all types of areas.

- This study exclusively uses the data from **144 consecutive residential property sales** from Brisbane real estate agency Cape Cod Residential.
- The sales cover a **broad range of locations** (more than 60 Greater Brisbane suburbs), a broad range of residential **property types** (apartments, townhomes and houses) and a broad range of **prices** ($375,000 to $3,500,000) over a 6-year period starting at January 2015 until December 2020.
- All properties received **the same consistent and uniform set of services.**
- Each property received:
  - A full home staging service,
  - The same photographer and photographic package,
  - The same marketing package,
  - The same pricing strategy (i.e. un-priced or 'For Sale'),
  - The same method of sale (private treaty), and
  - The same small sales team and negotiation strategy.
- It is important to note that one of the greatest hurdles most sellers face when selecting a home staging or property styling service is the overall cost of the exercise. Cape Cod Residential was able to eliminate this hurdle and **ensure the integrity** of the study results due to the fact that Cape Cod Residential provided their own in-house designer-quality furniture and accessory inventory, and own in-house professional property stylists, to every client at no hire charge or styling charge. **Cape Cod Residential's unique business model of fully-integrated real estate sales and property styling (all-inclusive staging, styling and selling) ensured that every home within the study sample size of 144 received high-calibre home staging/property styling.**

"AVERAGE DAYS-ON-MARKET ACROSS THE ENTIRE STUDY PERIOD WAS **JUST 14 DAYS**"

THE IMPACT ON SALES SPEED

The Australian Experience

Graph 1.1 The Time It Took Cape Cod Residential To Sell Most Homes

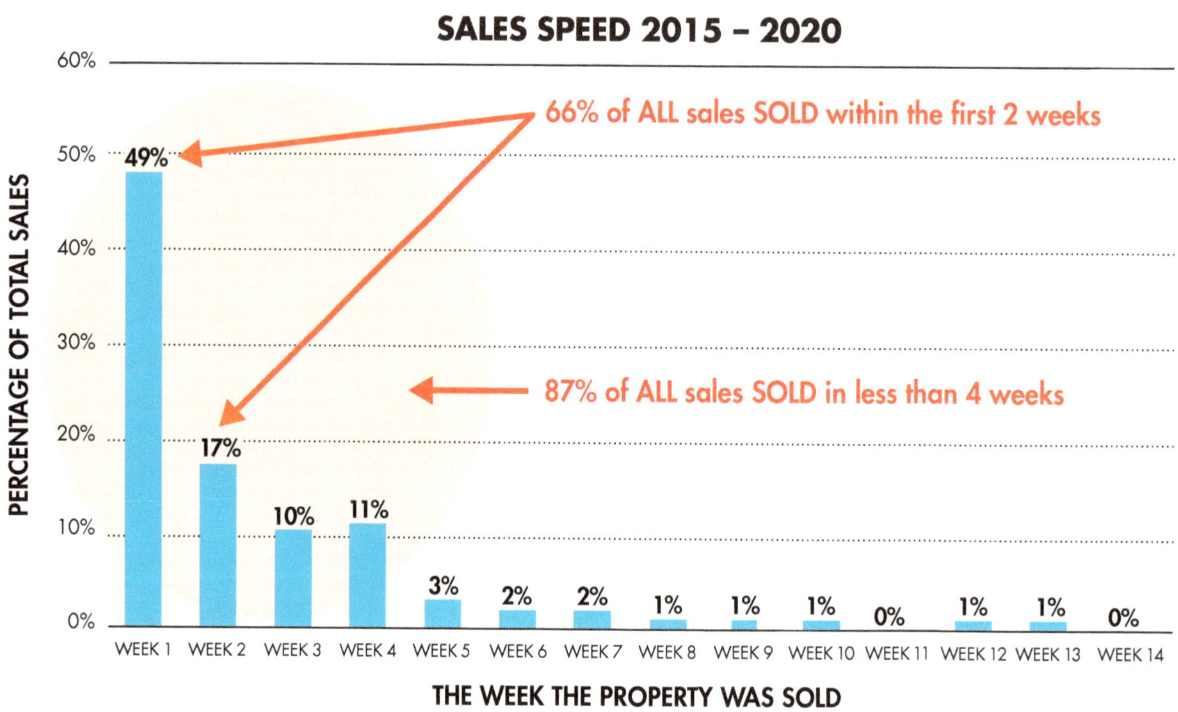

While almost all homes (87%) were sold within the first month that each property was on the market, the majority of homes (66%) were sold within 14 days of the first open home. Extraordinarily, **almost half (49%) of all properties were sold within the first week of the property being on the market.**

The study's consistently fast sales results also validate the study's frequent and strong price results, for the simple reason that homeowners are hesitant to accept early price offers unless the price is highly attractive and recognised as significantly above-market.

Graph 1.2 Annual Average and Median Days-On-Market

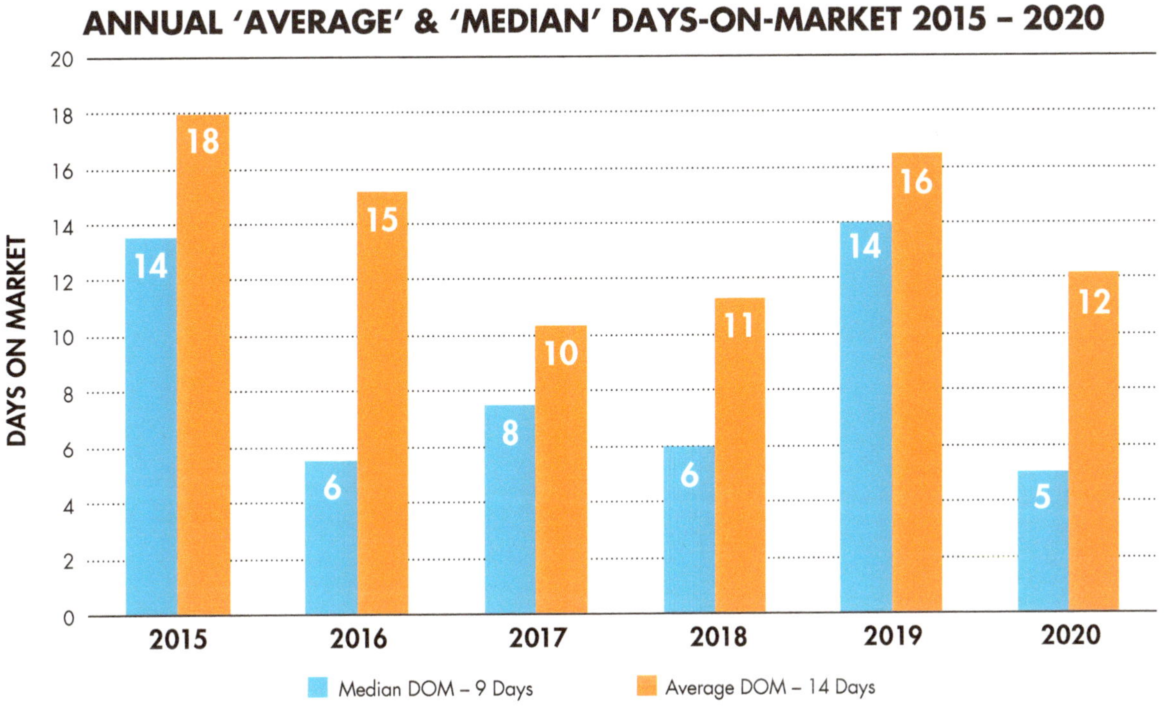

There are differing points of view across the property industry in relation to the merits of using 'sales success rates' derived from the **'average' days-on-market** metric **versus** the use of the **'median' days-on-market** metric.

In order to eliminate any bias from the selective use of one metric over the other, and in order to show the strong basis for the conclusions in this study, the results outlined in graph 1.2 above show that **both** the 'average' and the 'median' days-on-market metrics **reflect the same level of 'sales speed' consistency**.

Graph 1.3 Days-On-Market versus Annual Sales and Suburb Numbers

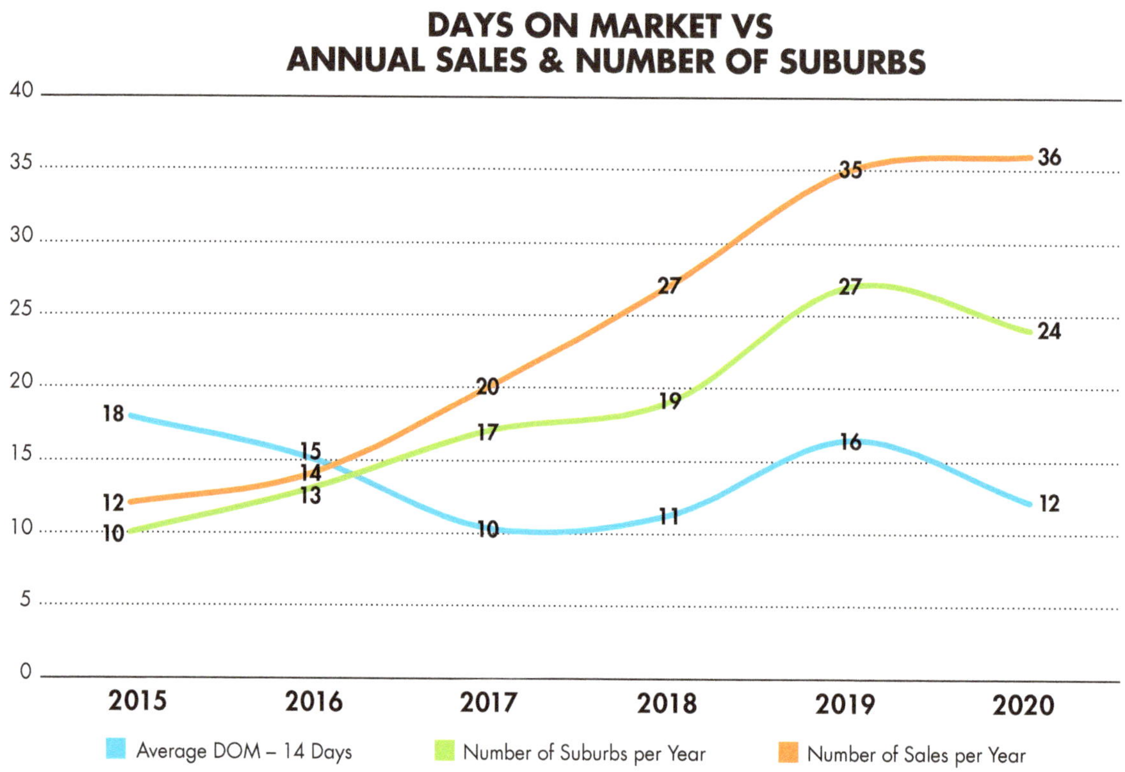

The **evidence** that a presentation-centric sales approach significantly decreases the time a property takes to sell can be seen in graph 1.3 above.

As the number of sales, and the number of suburbs (and therefore different types of homes), increases each year, the average days on market remains almost unchanged.

Graph 1.4 Greater Brisbane Average Days-On-Market versus Cape Cod Residential Days-On-Market

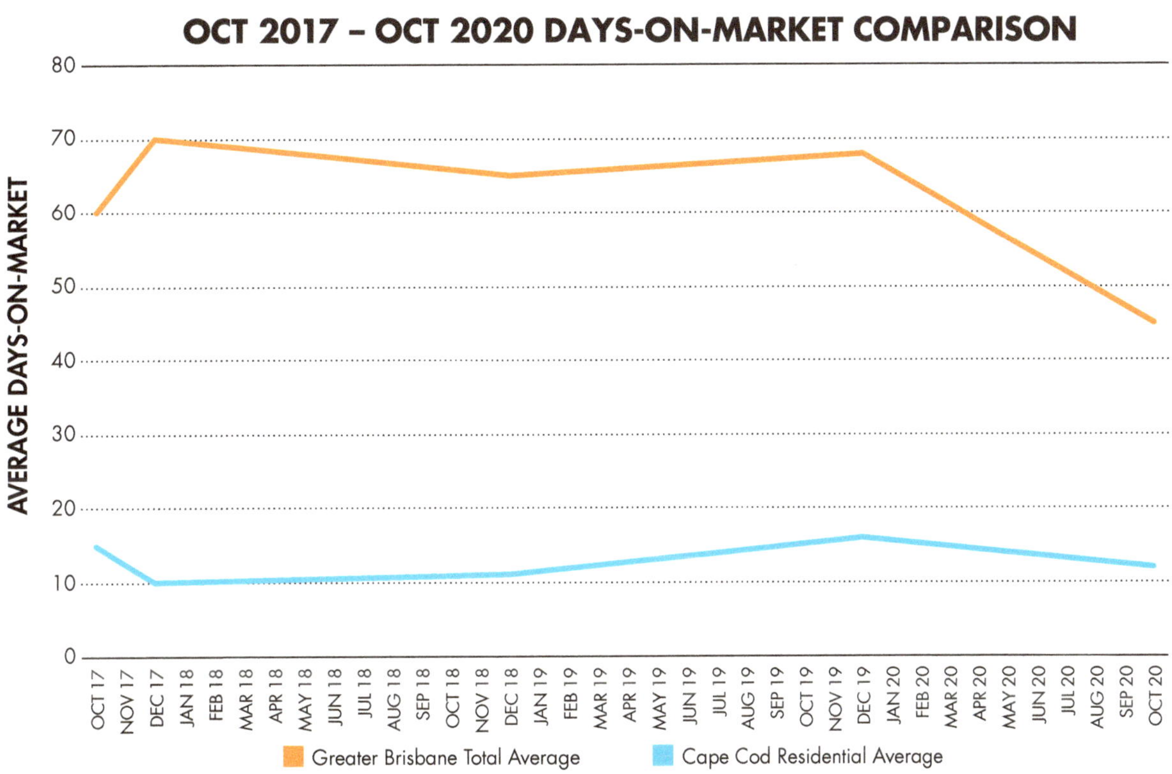

Source: Greater Brisbane Data – Corelogic

Graph 1.4 above also shows the significant, and beneficial, improvement that a consistently utilised, high-calibre, presentation-centric sales process makes with respect to sales timeframes.

An analysis of the market data of all real estate agents in the Greater Brisbane area for the 2-year period of January 2019 to January 2021 provides **additional evidence** of the statistically significant impact of high-calibre property styling on sales time frames.

As at 31 January 2021 there were 2788 real estate agents in the Greater Brisbane area (according to the REA Group who own and operate www.realestate.com.au) where approximately 86% (2,400+) of these agents had median days-on-market results of 30 to 120+ days during the 2-year analysis period. Conversely, Anne-Maree Russell, the Principal and Creative Director of Cape Cod Residential, sold 45 properties (as lead agent) over this 2-year period in a median days-on-market timeframe of just 9 days. In fact, **no other agent in Greater Brisbane sold more properties (as a lead agent) at a faster rate over this same period.**

The International Experience

62% of American selling agents in the 2017 survey of 1,894 real estate agents by America's largest association of real estate agents, The National Association of Realtors, stated that **home staging decreased the amount of time a home was on the market**.

A recent RESA (Real Estate Staging Association of North America and Canada) **study of 634 homes that were 'staged', detailed that these staged homes sold at an average speed of just 18 Days On Market.** This was in stark contrast to homes that weren't staged selling at an average speed of over 100 Days On Market.

In addition, RESA's 2020 survey of 13,000 'staged' homes across the USA illustrated the significant benefit that home staging makes as the **average time to sell the 13,000 staged homes was just 23 days!**

THE IMPACT ON SALES PRICES

The Australian Experience

Graph 2.1 The Distribution Of Price Premiums

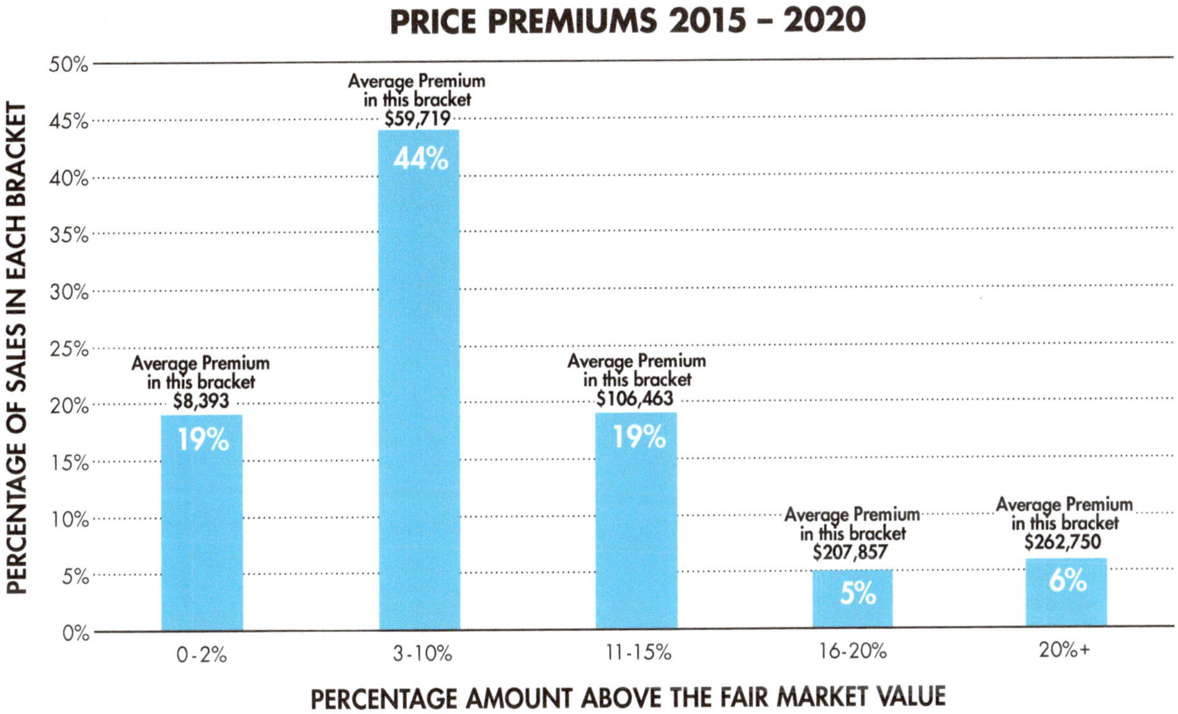

Price Premiums are the difference between the market value of a property and the final sales price. Price Premiums were calculated based upon the combined **written pre-market comparable sales analysis**/valuation and/or online *sort price and the final price as outlined on the contract of sale.

The average increase in the final sales price across the homes in this study **was $69,017**, with the bulk of sales price premiums falling into the **range of the 3%-10%** price premium bracket.

Almost one third (30%) of all home sales achieved a price premium of approximately **$100,000 or more.**

**NB the 'sort price' is the price that's listed behind the scenes on the online property listing portals such as www.realestate.com.au or www.domain.com.au.*

Graph 2.2 The Consistency Of Price Premiums

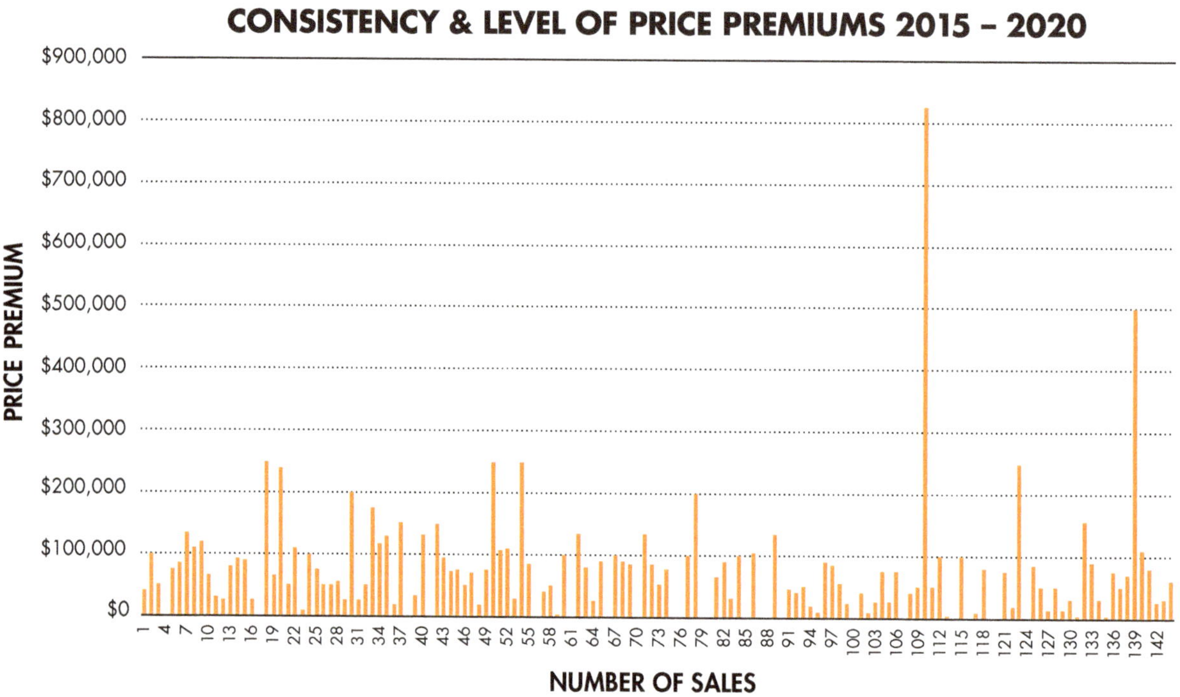

The consistent number of home sellers who experienced a price premium above the market value of their home, becomes apparent when examining the data in Graph 2.2 above.

Approximately **85% of all homes** in this study experienced a final sales price that was an **above-market result,** which is a testament to the beneficial impact of high-calibre property styling.

> "THE MAJORITY OF HOMES WERE SOLD FOR PRICES **3-10% ABOVE** THEIR MARKET VALUE"

The International Experience

The **Real Estate Staging Association** 2020 survey of 'staged' homes across the USA illustrated that **85% of the 13,000 homes** included in the survey **sold for prices 5-23% over their listing price.**

In a 2017 survey conducted by the **National Association of Realtors,** 50% of seller's agents in the survey of 1,894 agents stated that **home staging provided a 1%-10% increase in the final sales price** of the homes they were selling.

THE IMPACT ON BUYER INTEREST

The Australian Experience

Above-average open home attendance (commonly 50-100 attendees) at the initial open home, and superior views and enquiries (in comparison to local area listings*) for each campaign, provide additional weight to the argument that high-calibre property styling significantly increases the level of buyer interest for all types of property campaigns.

Graph 3.1 Buyer Interest Metrics

EXAMPLE CAMPAIGN 'BUYER INTEREST' METRICS

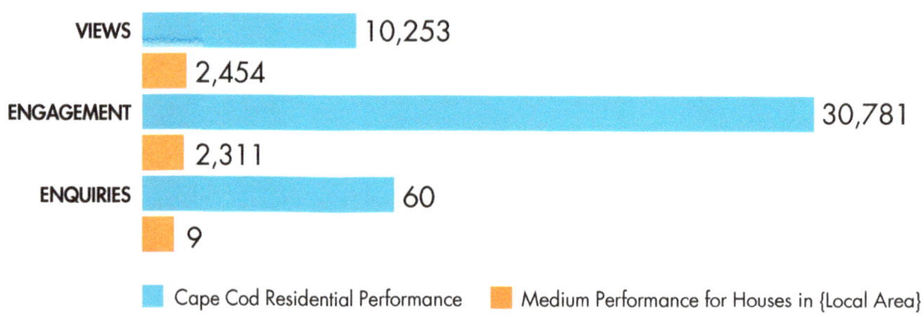

Superior performance for 'buyer interest' metrics (similar to the metrics outlined in graph 3.1 above) was exhibited for 100% of the 144 sales detailed in this study when compared to the local area performance.

**Campaign 'buyer interest' data was obtained for each sale in this study from Corelogic and is retained by the authors.*

The International Experience

The 2017 survey of 1,894 real estate agents by America's largest association of real estate agents, **The National Association of Realtors**, illustrated that **home staging had an impact, or effect, on up to 96% of a buyer's opinion**, or view of a home.

This same survey outlined that **77% of buyers agents said that home staging made it easier for a buyer to visualize a property** as a future home.

> "The body of evidence in this study conclusively illustrates that **CONSISTENTLY SUPERIOR SALES RESULTS** can be expected when agents use a **PRESENTATION-CENTRIC SALES PROCESS**"

COMMENTARY & CONCLUSIONS

Property Styling (often termed Home Staging) has grown in popularity in Australia over the past 10 years. The concept of renting 'display furniture' for the purpose of selling a home has its commercial origins in places like the USA, with organisations such as the Real Estate Staging Association (RESA) now having thousands of home stagers in their membership group.

Australian home owners have recognised the merits of staging a home for sale, and as such, there are many hundreds of home staging/property styling firms throughout Australia providing furniture, accessories and styling services to home owners who have recognised that well-presented homes sell faster and sell for higher prices.

Although it is widely accepted that staging and styling a property for the purposes of sale has the potential to provide a commercial benefit to any Australian homeowner, **the exact magnitude and scope of the benefits has remained relatively subjective and unknown due to the lack of objective studies, surveys or data collection**.

This observational study is designed to deliver objective, evidence-based information about the exact benefits home sellers can expect from a high-calibre property styling sales methodology.

As the Australian pioneers of the new and progressive real estate model, all-inclusive Staging, Styling and Selling, Cape Cod Residential was uniquely qualified to assess the impact of high-calibre property styling on residential property sales.

Every homeowner in this study was provided with access to Cape Cod Residential's in-house designer-quality furniture and accessory inventory and professional property stylists. Most importantly, **every property in the study received an unrestrained full home staging service**. This was only possible due to the distinctively unique Cape Cod Residential business model which universally integrates 'no cost' inventory hire, and 'no cost' property styling, as part of every seller's real estate experience.

Ensuring that every home was fully staged and styled provided a **unique level of integrity** to the results in this study as it overcame the most common objection to staging and styling a home ... **the high costs of professional home staging**.

It is also important to note that regardless of the nature, location or price point of each property the same sales methodology and level of home staging was utilised.

In addition, in spite of the fact that all sales used a private treaty sales methodology (i.e. no auctions), did not use any print media or professional video productions and did not require any other 'technological' promotional tools, the sales speeds and price premiums across the sales in this study, were significantly better than market comparisons.

The **evidence in this observational analysis** clearly shows a **clear and concise positive correlation between high-calibre property styling and high-performance sales results.**

While the evidence outlined in this study illustrates the distinct and powerful commercial benefit high-calibre home staging/property styling can provide to almost any home seller, it needs to be noted that the **results in this study may not be the same from agency to agency.**

Not all real estate agents have equivalent negotiation skills or interpersonal communication techniques and **not all real estate agents will achieve the same results as those in this analysis.**

However, while results may vary from agent to agent, **the body of evidence within this study conclusively illustrates that consistently superior sales results can be expected** across the majority of residential home types and geographical locations when real estate agents consistently utilize a presentation-centric sales process.

LIST OF SALES

PROPERTY TYPE	SUBURB	BEDS	SOLD DATE	SOLD PRICE	WEEK SOLD
House	BALMORAL	4	9/02/2015	$890,000	SOLD IN WEEK 2
Townhouse	BULIMBA	3	19/05/2015	$900,000	SOLD IN WEEK 1
House	CARINDALE	4	17/06/2015	$750,000	SOLD IN WEEK 3
Townhouse	BULIMBA	3	15/06/2015	$835,000	SOLD IN WEEK 2
House	ASHGROVE	4	22/05/2015	$925,000	SOLD IN WEEK 3
House	NORMAN PARK	3	3/08/2015	$835,000	SOLD IN WEEK 1
House	ORMISTON	4	23/07/2015	$1,035,000	SOLD IN WEEK 4
House	BIRKDALE	4	3/09/2015	$1,310,000	SOLD IN WEEK 5
House	SEVEN HILLS	3	21/11/2015	$820,000	SOLD IN WEEK 1
Townhouse	WEST END	3	22/11/2015	$915,000	SOLD IN WEEK 5
Townhouse	BULIMBA	3	26/10/2015	$810,000	SOLD IN WEEK 9
House	MACKENZIE	4	8/11/2015	$725,000	SOLD IN WEEK 2
House	WAKERLEY	5	12/02/2016	$881,000	SOLD IN WEEK 1
House	ALDERLEY	6	25/02/2016	$1,042,000	SOLD IN WEEK 2
House	TARINGA	5	7/05/2016	$1,390,000	SOLD IN WEEK 12
House	TINGALPA	4	21/05/2016	$525,000	SOLD IN WEEK 1
House	CAMP HILL	5	31/05/2016	$1,750,000	SOLD IN WEEK 4
House	CAMP HILL	5	12/06/2016	$1,250,000	SOLD IN WEEK 1
Townhouse	HAWTHORNE	4	12/06/2016	$915,000	SOLD IN WEEK 8
House	CARINDALE	5	21/07/2016	$1,240,000	SOLD IN WEEK 1
House	WINDSOR	2	6/08/2016	$725,000	SOLD IN WEEK 1
House	WYNNUM	4	7/09/2016	$1,010,000	SOLD IN WEEK 1
House	CALAMVALE	4	29/09/2016	$610,000	SOLD IN WEEK 1
House	SEVEN HILLS	5	29/10/2016	$1,600,000	SOLD IN WEEK 1
Apartment	HIGHGATE HILL	3	21/11/2016	$825,800	SOLD IN WEEK 2
House	COORPAROO	3	1/12/2016	$800,000	SOLD IN WEEK 2
House	CORINDA	3	14/02/2017	$1,000,000	SOLD IN WEEK 4
House	CANNON HILL	3	18/02/2017	$755,000	SOLD IN WEEK 1
House	EAST BRISBANE	4	20/02/2017	$877,000	SOLD IN WEEK 3
House	ALBION	4	25/02/2017	$1,200,000	SOLD IN WEEK 1
House	CALAMVALE	4	18/03/2017	$625,000	SOLD IN WEEK 1
House	NUNDAH	4	8/04/2017	$1,001,000	SOLD IN WEEK 1
House	CORINDA	5	22/04/2017	$1,125,000	SOLD IN WEEK 1
House	CARINDALE	5	7/05/2017	$1,067,000	SOLD IN WEEK 1
House	CAMP HILL	5	28/05/2017	$1,130,000	SOLD IN WEEK 3
House	CARINA	4	22/06/2017	$920,000	SOLD IN WEEK 1

PROPERTY TYPE	SUBURB	BEDS	SOLD DATE	SOLD PRICE	WEEK SOLD
House	FIG TREE POCKET	5	23/06/2017	$1,350,000	SOLD IN WEEK 2
Apartment	HOLLAND PARK WEST	3	5/07/2017	$850,000	SOLD IN WEEK 2
House	CAMP HILL	5	16/07/2017	$933,000	SOLD IN WEEK 2
House	UPPER MOUNT GRAVATT	3	25/07/2017	$732,000	SOLD IN WEEK 1
House	HAWTHORNE	4	13/08/2017	$1,590,000	SOLD IN WEEK 7
House	ASHGROVE	5	3/09/2017	$1,249,500	SOLD IN WEEK 2
House	RED HILL	2	9/09/2017	$795,000	SOLD IN WEEK 1
House	CAMP HILL	4	14/10/2017	$1,023,000	SOLD IN WEEK 1
House	HAWTHORNE	5	22/10/2017	$1,676,000	SOLD IN WEEK 2
House	BULIMBA	4	21/11/2017	$1,250,000	SOLD IN WEEK 5
House	CARINA HEIGHTS	5	14/01/2018	$1,170,000	SOLD IN WEEK 1
House	PARKINSON	4	3/02/2018	$530,000	SOLD IN WEEK 2
House	HENDRA	3	11/02/2018	$975,000	SOLD IN WEEK 1
Acreage/Semi-Rural	THORNLANDS	5	3/03/2018	$1,450,000	SOLD IN WEEK 1
House	WYNNUM	4	20/03/2018	$1,008,000	SOLD IN WEEK 1
House	INDOOROOPILLY	4	25/03/2018	$1,010,000	SOLD IN WEEK 1
House	CORINDA	3	26/03/2018	$629,000	SOLD IN WEEK 6
House	HOLLAND PARK	5	22/04/2018	$1,350,000	SOLD IN WEEK 1
House	CARINDALE	5	7/05/2018	$1,085,000	SOLD IN WEEK 1
House	UPPER MOUNT GRAVATT	5	19/05/2018	$850,000	SOLD IN WEEK 3
House	HOLLAND PARK	4	22/05/2018	$940,000	SOLD IN WEEK 4
House	CLAYFIELD	4	25/05/2018	$1,050,000	SOLD IN WEEK 1
House	MILTON	3	6/06/2018	$905,000	SOLD IN WEEK 4
House	ALDERLEY	3	22/06/2018	$900,000	SOLD IN WEEK 1
Townhouse	MORNINGSIDE	3	26/06/2018	$840,000	SOLD IN WEEK 6
House	WYNNUM	5	22/07/2018	$1,335,000	SOLD IN WEEK 2
House	JAMBOREE HEIGHTS	4	28/07/2018	$630,200	SOLD IN WEEK 1
House	NUNDAH	4	17/08/2018	$825,000	SOLD IN WEEK 2
House	WINDSOR	3	23/08/2018	$890,000	SOLD IN WEEK 1
House	WYNNUM	4	9/09/2018	$850,000	SOLD IN WEEK 2
House	COORPAROO	5	14/10/2018	$1,300,000	SOLD IN WEEK 1
House	NUNDAH	3	17/10/2018	$790,000	SOLD IN WEEK 1
House	WINDSOR	5	24/10/2018	$1,085,000	SOLD IN WEEK 3
House	HERSTON	5	14/11/2018	$1,680,000	SOLD IN WEEK 3
House	COORPAROO	5	23/11/2018	$1,335,000	SOLD IN WEEK 1
House	WINDSOR	5	2/12/2018	$1,035,000	SOLD IN WEEK 4

PROPERTY TYPE	SUBURB	BEDS	SOLD DATE	SOLD PRICE	WEEK SOLD
House	WINDSOR	4	5/12/2018	$1,052,000	SOLD IN WEEK 3
House	SALISBURY	3	30/01/2019	$677,000	SOLD IN WEEK 1
Land	NORMAN PARK	N/A	4/02/2019	$545,000	SOLD IN WEEK 12
House	CAMP HILL	5	13/02/2019	$1,750,000	SOLD IN WEEK 4
House	CARINDALE	5	13/02/2019	$1,100,000	SOLD IN WEEK 1
House	ASHGROVE	5	16/02/2019	$1,900,000	SOLD IN WEEK 1
House	WYNNUM	3	2/03/2019	$1,200,000	SOLD IN WEEK 4
House	MURARRIE	5	4/03/2019	$910,000	SOLD IN WEEK 2
Unit	ASCOT	3	11/03/2019	$515,000	SOLD IN WEEK 3
House	GORDON PARK	3	16/03/2019	$841,000	SOLD IN WEEK 1
House	COORPAROO	5	27/03/2019	$1,030,000	SOLD IN WEEK 3
House	CAMP HILL	5	24/04/2019	$1,100,000	SOLD IN WEEK 4
House	COORPAROO	5	3/05/2019	$1,300,000	SOLD IN WEEK 7
House	BULIMBA	4	5/05/2019	$1,705,000	SOLD IN WEEK 1
Terrace	KANGAROO POINT	4	8/05/2019	$1,400,000	SOLD IN WEEK 4
House	NORMAN PARK	4	30/05/2019	$1,275,000	SOLD IN WEEK 4
House	CLAYFIELD	4	1/06/2019	$1,535,000	SOLD IN WEEK 3
House	COORPAROO	4	3/06/2019	$1,250,000	SOLD IN WEEK 3
House	LAWNTON	4	23/06/2019	$495,000	SOLD IN WEEK 5
House	MANSFIELD	3	25/06/2019	$640,000	SOLD IN WEEK 1
House	CARINA HEIGHTS	5	11/07/2019	$1,050,000	SOLD IN WEEK 4
House	BIRKDALE	5	20/07/2019	$870,000	SOLD IN WEEK 2
Unit	ST LUCIA	3	23/07/2019	$810,000	SOLD IN WEEK 1
House	HOLLAND PARK WEST	5	9/08/2019	$1,240,000	SOLD IN WEEK 1
House	BULIMBA	5	1/09/2019	$1,585,000	SOLD IN WEEK 2
Unit	CLAYFIELD	2	22/09/2019	$405,000	SOLD IN WEEK 1
Unit	HAWTHORNE	2	27/09/2019	$453,000	SOLD IN WEEK 2
Townhouse	BALMORAL	3	13/10/2019	$790,000	SOLD IN WEEK 4
House	BARDON	3	15/10/2019	$840,000	SOLD IN WEEK 1
House	ORMISTON	4	21/10/2019	$610,000	SOLD IN WEEK 1
Unit	INDOOROOPILLY	2	11/11/2019	$375,000	SOLD IN WEEK 6
House	COORPAROO	5	18/11/2019	$925,000	SOLD IN WEEK 3
House	THE GAP	3	18/11/2019	$775,000	SOLD IN WEEK 1
House	UPPER MOUNT GRAVATT	5	23/11/2019	$925,000	SOLD IN WEEK 1
House	RED HILL	4	9/12/2019	$1,800,000	SOLD IN WEEK 5
Townhouse	CLAYFIELD	3	20/12/2019	$640,000	SOLD IN WEEK 2

PROPERTY TYPE	SUBURB	BEDS	SOLD DATE	SOLD PRICE	WEEK SOLD
House	WAVELL HEIGHTS	4	2/02/2020	$700,000	SOLD IN WEEK 1
House	CLAYFIELD	5	19/01/2020	$2,825,000	SOLD IN WEEK 1
House	WAVELL HEIGHTS	4	2/02/2020	$700,000	SOLD IN WEEK 1
House	HOLLAND PARK	5	16/02/2020	$1,450,000	SOLD IN WEEK 1
Townhouse	ANNERLEY	2	6/04/2020	$505,000	SOLD IN WEEK 4
House	CAPALABA	4	16/03/2020	$660,000	SOLD IN WEEK 4
Apartment	NEW FARM	2	27/03/2020	$1,400,000	SOLD IN WEEK 1
House	WAKERLEY	4	30/03/2020	$840,000	SOLD IN WEEK 4
House	CARINA	4	31/03/2020	$910,000	SOLD IN WEEK 2
House	WYNNUM	3	2/04/2020	$730,000	SOLD IN WEEK 2
Townhouse	ANNERLEY	3	1/05/2020	$610,000	SOLD IN WEEK 7
Apartment	NUNDAH	3	11/05/2020	$590,000	SOLD IN WEEK 1
Apartment	NUNDAH	3	16/05/2020	$390,000	SOLD IN WEEK 1
House	ASPLEY	4	1/06/2020	$720,000	SOLD IN WEEK 2
House	GRACEVILLE	5	2/06/2020	$1,850,000	SOLD IN WEEK 2
Acreage/Semi-Rural	PULLENVALE	5	12/06/2020	$1,280,000	SOLD IN WEEK 13
House	NUNDAH	3	18/07/2020	$685,000	SOLD IN WEEK 1
House	CLAYFIELD	4	20/07/2020	$1,550,000	SOLD IN WEEK 3
House	WAVELL HEIGHTS	4	20/07/2020	$805,000	SOLD IN WEEK 1
House	CLAYFIELD	4	20/07/2020	$1,550,000	SOLD IN WEEK 3
House	WAVELL HEIGHTS	4	20/07/2020	$805,000	SOLD IN WEEK 1
House	CHERMSIDE	5	27/07/2020	$930,000	SOLD IN WEEK 1
House	CLAYFIELD	4	14/08/2020	$1,100,000	SOLD IN WEEK 5
House	CLAYFIELD	4	30/08/2020	$955,000	SOLD IN WEEK 1
House	WAKERLEY	5	3/09/2020	$890,000	SOLD IN WEEK 1
Townhouse	CANNON HILL	3	10/09/2020	$530,000	SOLD IN WEEK 1
House	CLAYFIELD	4	14/09/2020	$1,100,000	SOLD IN WEEK 10
House	CARINDALE	5	18/09/2020	$965,000	SOLD IN WEEK 1
House	MOUNT GRAVATT EAST	4	21/09/2020	$900,000	SOLD IN WEEK 1
Apartment	SOUTH BRISBANE	2	1/11/2020	$1,020,000	SOLD IN WEEK 1
House	WINDSOR	5	15/10/2020	$3,500,000	SOLD IN WEEK 1
House	ANNERLEY	5	22/11/2020	$1,200,000	SOLD IN WEEK 1
Townhouse	YERONGA	2	20/11/2020	$430,000	SOLD IN WEEK 1
House	CAMP HILL	4	1/12/2020	$1,000,000	SOLD IN WEEK 2
House	NORMAN PARK	5	3/12/2020	$1,630,000	SOLD IN WEEK 1
House	RED HILL	4	6/12/2020	$861,000	SOLD IN WEEK 1

ABOUT THE AUTHORS

Cape Cod Residential

Cape Cod Residential's achievements in the property styling field are unmatched by any other Australian real estate agency or any other Australian Home Staging/Property Styling firm.

As the winner of the RESA (North American Real Estate Staging Association) 2020 International Home Stager of The Year Award (vacant homes) and the winner of 8 Housing Industry of Australia Property Styling awards for the last 5 consecutive years (2016-2020), including the 2020 QLD Property Styling Project Of The Year, **Cape Cod Residential is widely recognised as Australia's pre-eminent real estate presentation specialist.**

Cape Cod Residential is also the founder of The Australian Real eStagents® Network and is owned and operated by Luke and Anne-Maree Russell. Anne-Maree was also one of just 4 finalists for the Gold REA Award for 'Most Influential Woman in Property' at the 2019 National REA Excellence Awards.

In 2019 Cape Cod Residential also published their highly acclaimed seller-centric educational books **Price Truths** and **Negotiation Truths,** in an effort to enhance the 'advisory' profile of the real estate profession.

Anne-Maree is one of the most followed social media influencers in the real estate space across her multiple Instagram and Facebook accounts and can be found at the following accounts:

Instagram accounts:
@capecodresidential,
@capecodresidentialstyling, and
@thenexthousethatambuilt

Web: www.capecodresidential.com.au
Email:: sales@capecodresidential.com.au

RESA 2020 HOME STAGING INDUSTRY AWARDS
HOME STAGER OF THE YEAR VACANT INTERNATIONAL
Anne-Maree Russell

WINNER 2020 HIA & IDA Qld Property Styling Small Residential

WINNER 2020 HIA & IDA Qld Property Styling Large Residential

WINNER 2020 HIA & IDA Qld Property Styling Project Of The Year

2016 2017 2018 2019 2020
MULTI-AWARD WINNING PROPERTY STYLING

HIA MEMBER

The IDA – Interior Design Association

Established some 15 years ago, and formally known as QIDA (Queensland Interior Decorators Association), The Interior Design Association (IDA) was formally registered under the new name and brand in March 2020, with the aim of creating a national representative body for the Interior Design industry.

The IDA, is a dynamic, supportive membership group of Design Professionals (Interior Designers, Interior Decorators, Interior Stylists) and industry associates from the Retail, Building and Construction industries.

Our members are qualified and highly skilled professionals ready to assist with a wide range of commercial or residential interior design and styling services.

Working within a like-minded network of industry partners, IDA members have access to current industry practice information on products, services and innovations.

You can be assured when you hire an IDA Design Professional, you will be working with someone with interior design training (and/or extensive professional experience) who has the passion and desire to exceed their client's expectations.

Contact: 1300 768 054 | Web: www.theida.org.au | Email: home@theida.org.au
www.facebook.com/interiordesignassociation/ | www.instagram.com/ida_designassociation/

www.ingramcontent.com/pod-product-compliance
Ingram Content Group UK Ltd.
Pitfield, Milton Keynes, MK11 3LW, UK
UKHW061959290726
14090UKWH00021B/1289

9 781639 019977